BUILDING A ROMAN FORT

By Robin Twiddy

LIFE LONG AGO

BookLife
PUBLISHING

©2019
BookLife Publishing Ltd.
King's Lynn
Norfolk PE30 4LS

ISBN: 978-1-78637-547-6

Written by:
Robin Twiddy

Edited by:
Emilie Dufresne

Designed by:
Danielle Jones

IMAGE CREDITS

CONTENTS

Words that look like THIS can be found in the glossary on page 24.

The ROMANS in BRITAIN

Hi, my name is Atticus and the year is <u>A.D.</u> 46. My dad is a <u>CENTURION</u> in the Roman army. That means he is in charge of 80 soldiers. We are going to build a fort; a fort is a place for soldiers to live and defend an area from enemies.

We Romans first <u>INVADED</u> Britain in 55 <u>B.C.</u>

4

First, we need to pick a <u>STRATEGIC</u> place for our fort.
Over there looks good! It is near to the village and on a hill.
That means it will be harder to attack, and we will be able
to see a long way.

All Roman forts are built from the same basic plans. They are then changed depending on where the fort is.

PERIMETER

All Roman forts are built in a very large rectangle with rounded corners. But the first thing we need to do is dig a ditch. Every Roman fort has a deep ditch all the way round.

The ditch will make it hard for FOOT SOLDIERS to attack.

We use the dirt from the ditch and some heavy stones to build a rampart. Sometimes we put sharp sticks into the ditch. This can make it very dangerous to attack our walls.

This is the top of the rampart where the wall and <u>PARAPET</u> will be built.

A rampart is a defensive wall with walkways.

The rampart has a slope that is made with dirt from the ditch.

This is the trench.

Some Roman forts only last a short time before being taken down. These are built with wood instead of concrete.

Rampart

Now it's time to build the walls. We are building our walls to about seven and a half metres high. Can you see those parts that stick up at the top? They will protect us from arrows if we are attacked.

Now the walls are up, we will need to be able to get in and out. A Roman fort has four entrances; one on each side. In large forts, each entrance has two gates.

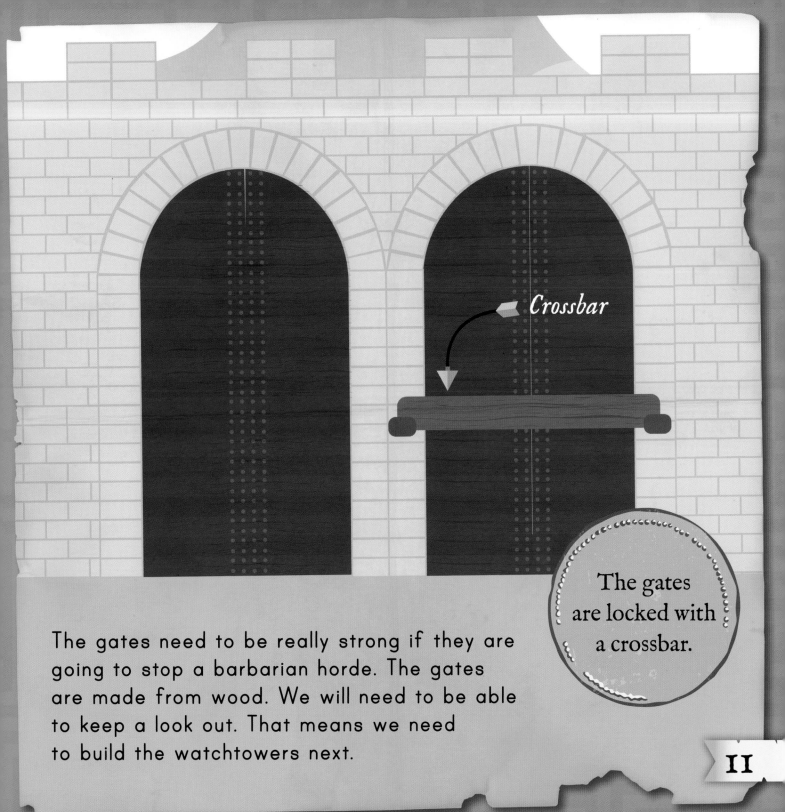

Crossbar

The gates are locked with a crossbar.

The gates need to be really strong if they are going to stop a barbarian horde. The gates are made from wood. We will need to be able to keep a look out. That means we need to build the watchtowers next.

WATCHTOWERS

The watchtowers will be about nine metres high. We need one either side of each gate and one in each corner. If the fort is really large, we can add one in the middle of each of the longer walls.

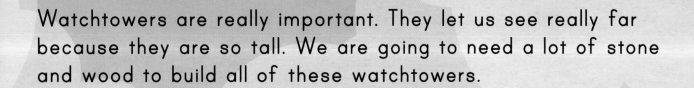

Watchtowers are really important. They let us see really far because they are so tall. We are going to need a lot of stone and wood to build all of these watchtowers.

Now that the fort has strong defences, we should work on the inside. The soldiers will need somewhere to sleep!

BARRACKS

The barracks is where the soldiers sleep and cook their meals. We will need ten blocks of barracks, like this. This will hold a century of men – that means 80. The commander, my dad, will have his own building.

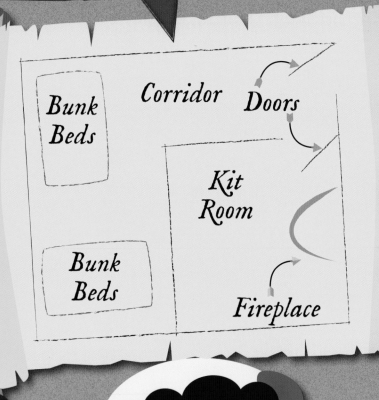

Each bedroom will hold eight men on bunk beds and has a room for them to keep their equipment in. It is important that the barracks are close to the gates so that the soldiers can defend the fort in a hurry.

The soldiers will organise the barracks how it suits them best.

PRINCIPIA

There are two main roads in a Roman fort. These join the four gates in a cross. They meet outside the principia. The principia is the biggest and most important building in the fort.

Principia

Gates

Roads

All roads lead to the principia!

The principia is where the money to pay the soldiers is kept. It is also the shrine for the fort – this is where everyone will come to pray. Lots of important business and planning will take place in here.

This is the headquarters for the fort.

PRAETORIUM

Now we have somewhere for the commander or general to plan and give orders. But he and his family will need somewhere to live. We had better build the praetorium next then. The praetorium is much fancier than the barracks!

Only rich and important people can become commanders in the Roman army. The praetorium has room for the commander and his family and their servants. Soldiers from the lower ranks are not allowed to marry.

This is where I will live with my mum and dad, because my dad is the commander!

OTHER BUILDINGS

It says in the plans that there are a few more buildings to add. We need a horreum. This is a warehouse to keep grain and food. A fabricae should be built over there. That's a workshop for making tools, weapons and armour.

Oh, and we'd better not forget the public toilets. We will need to dig a long trench and carve a long wooden bench with holes in it. Ah here comes Gaius with the <u>COMMUNAL</u> sponge for the toilets. Don't ask what it's for!

Finished JUST in TIME

Wow, our fort looks great. If we were building a bigger fort, we could add some shops. Maybe we could even build a <u>ROMAN BATH</u>. We should probably build that outside the fort. They have a tendency to catch fire because of the <u>FURNACE</u>.

Here come the Celts! It's time to test the defences. I think they are going to have trouble getting past the ditches and ramparts! The parapet should protect us from their arrows. Romans – defensive positions!

23

GLOSSARY

A.D.	meaning 'in the year of the lord', it marks the year that Jesus was born and is used as the starting year for most calendars
B.C.	meaning 'before Christ', it is used to mark dates that occurred before the starting year of most calendars
centurion	the commander of a century of Roman soldiers
communal	shared or used by a group or community
foot soldiers	soldiers who travel and attack on foot without horse or cart
furnace	a structure that is used to heat a Roman bath
invaded	having attacked and taken control of a country
parapet	a low defensive wall along a walkway
Roman bath	a building with rooms for bathing, relaxing and socialising with baths of water and steam
strategic	plans or actions with over-all long-term military goals in mind
volcanic	relating to volcanoes

INDEX